GLASS WINGS

Fleur Adcock was born in New Zealand in 1934. She spent the war years in England, returning with her family to New Zealand in 1947. She emigrated to Britain in 1963, working as a librarian in London until 1979. In 1977-78 she was writer-in-residence at Charlotte Mason College of Education, Ambleside. She was Northern Arts Literary Fellow in 1979-81, living in Newcastle, becoming a freelance writer after her return to London. She received an OBE in 1996, and the Queen's Gold Medal for Poetry in 2006 for *Poems 1960-2000* (Bloodaxe Books, 2000).

Fleur Adcock published three pamphlets with Bloodaxe: *Below Loughrigg* (1979), *Hotspur* (1986) and *Meeting the Comet* (1988), as well as her translations of medieval Latin lyrics, *The Virgin & the Nightingale* (1983). All her other collections were published by Oxford University Press until they shut down their poetry list in 1999, after which Bloodaxe published her collected poems, *Poems 1960-2000* (2000), followed by *Dragon Talk* in 2010 and *Glass Wings* in 2013.

FLEUR ADCOCK

GLASS
WINGS

BLOODAXE BOOKS

First published 2013 in the UK by
Bloodaxe Books Ltd,
Highgreen,
Tarset,
Northumberland NE48 1RP
and by Victoria University Press
in New Zealand.

www.bloodaxebooks.com
For further information about Bloodaxe titles
please visit our website or write to
the above address for a catalogue.

Supported by
**ARTS COUNCIL
ENGLAND**

Cover design: Neil Astley & Pamela Robertson-Pearce.

Printed in Great Britain by
Bell & Bain Limited, Glasgow, Scotland.

For Gregory and Andrew

ACKNOWLEDGEMENTS

Acknowledgements are due to the editors of the following publications in which some of these poems first appeared: *Agenda*, *Ambit*, *The Guardian*, *Magma*, *New Zealand Books*, *PN Review*, *Poetry London*, *Poetry Review*, *The Poetry Paper*, *The Rialto*, *The RSPB Anthology of Wildlife Poetry*, *The Spectator*, *The Times Literary Supplement*, and *The Yellow Nib*.

'For Michael at 70' was commissioned by Robin Robertson for *Love Poet, Carpenter: Michael Longley at Seventy* (Enitharmon, 2009); 'An 80th Birthday Card for Roy' was commissioned by Peter Robinson for *An Unofficial Roy Fisher* (Shearsman Books, 2010); 'The Translator' was written for *KJV: Old Text, New Poetry* (Wivenbooks, 2011); 'The Royal Visit' was commissioned by Carol Ann Duffy for *Jubilee Lines* (Faber, 2012).

CONTENTS

9   At the Crossing
10   For Michael at 70
11   An 80th Birthday Card for Roy
13   Finding Elizabeth Rainbow
14   Spuggies
15   Fox
16   The Saucer
17   The Belly Dancer
18   Ingeburg
20   Alfred
21   Match Girl
22   Alumnae Notes
23   Nominal Aphasia
24   Walking Stick
25   Macular Degeneration
26   Mrs Baldwin
27   Charon
28   Having Sex with the Dead

     TESTATORS
30   Robert Harington, 1558
31   Anthony Cave, 1558
32   Alice Adcock, 1673
33   Luke Sharpe, 1704
34   William Clayton, 1725
35   James Heyes, 1726
36   Henry Eggington, 1912
38   William Dick Mackley
40   The Translator
44   Intestate

     CAMPBELLS
47   Elegy for Alistair
48   Port Charles
49   What the 1950s Were Like
50   The Royal Visit

51 The Professor of Music
52 Coconut Matting
53 Epithalamium
54 A Novelty

MY LIFE WITH ARTHROPODS
56 Wet feet
57 Dung Beetle
58 Caterpillars
59 Stag Beetle
60 Praying Mantis
61 Flea
62 Hoppy
63 To the Mosquitoes of Auckland
64 Stick Insects
65 Crayfish
66 Slaters
67 Ella's Crane-flies
68 Orb Web
70 My Grubby Little Secret
71 In Provence
72 Unmentionable
73 Phobia
74 Blowflies
75 Bat Soup
76 Lepidoptera
78 Bees' Nest
79 Dragonfly

At the Crossing

The tall guy in a green T-shirt,
vanishing past me as I cross
in the opposite direction,
has fairy wings on his shoulders:
toy ones, children's fancy-dress wings,
cartoonish butterfly cut-outs.

Do they say gay? No time for that.
He flickers past the traffic lights –
whoosh! gone! – outside categories.
Do they say foreign? They say young.
They say London. Grab it, they say.
Kiss the winged joy as it flies.

Traffic swings around the corner;
gusts of drizzle sweep us along
the Strand in the glittering dark,
threading to and fro among skeins
of never-quite-colliding blurs.
All this whirling's why we came out.

Those fragile flaps could lift no one.
Perhaps they were ironic wings,
tongue-in-cheek look-at-me tokens
to make it clear he had no need
of hydraulics, being himself
Hermes.
          Wings, though; definite wings.

For Michael at 70

(Michael Longley, 2009)

I wish I had a gift for you to match
those packets of ghosts I used to send you
when I was teasing out your ancestry:

the Kentish farmers in their Wealden hamlets;
your great-grandfather, the 'Wood Reeve' –
or 'Peasant' (no apparent irony)

on a certificate; his son Charles Longley,
born in chocolate-box Chiddingstone, married
in Lambeth, propelled there by history.

It urged them all to London, in the end –
these, and your tobacco pipe makers
from Bucks – to change their lives, and link up with

your other lines: the Dorset brickmakers
(who must have talked, we think, like William Barnes),
and from Somerset the horsehair weaver

Henrietta (whose farm servant mother
her master took advantage of, she hints);
and that arch-Londoner and shape-shifter

William Braham: son of an engraver
born who knows where, and himself an artist,
jeweller, commission agent in the City,

pawnbroker – (conman, I suspect) – fit forbear
for your artist daughter, or for anyone
in the risky trickster trade of poetry.

They flit among their demolished streets, dodge
into unlit doorways, or slither behind
a hedge or haystack. They are shy of us.

All I can do is call them up again
to marvel at the poet they've produced.
Here are your ancestors. They don't explain you.

An 80th Birthday Card for Roy

(Roy Fisher, 2010)

Happy birthday! I'm sorry this is not
that clutch of long-tailed tits you always wanted
or a melodious charm of goldfinches.
They would certainly fly more gracefully
than my stumbling public-private poem
(you know how tricky such commissions are –
although you'd bring to them your customary
elegance, intelligence and wit).

In any case, you're doing all right for birds:
swallows dashing out from under your eaves,
thrushes and a blackbird both nesting
outside your kitchen window.
                    Here, I see,
I should slip in a flattering metaphor
about your lyric voice. It wouldn't be apt:
your poems are not songs; they are to think with.
Thank you for them; and not for them only.

I could start reminiscing – Arvon courses,
Bucharest, Burton Dassett, the Marsden hat –
but you know all that; and it's your birthday.
Happiness, we've agreed, tends more and more
these days to be bird-shaped. For a present,
if I can manage teleportation,
I'll zoom a pair of kingfishers your way;
or a golden oriole; a Phoenix.

Finding Elizabeth Rainbow

(i.m.)

Elizabeth Rainbow was lurking under the earth
a few yards from the west door. Someone
had scratched a window into the shallow turf
over her fallen gravestone. I called to Joyce –

Joyce was alive then – and she went to fetch you,
halfway to the car (you could still walk then).
You plodded back, this time with a gait
that almost demanded the word 'sprightly'.

That woman with the posse of children called them –
the little gigglers, the skinny black girl,
the teenager with cornflowers on his straw hat –
and they scrabbled at the soil like a pack of terriers.

Elizabeth was nestled into the ground
like the church itself, with its organically
sloping floor. We'd given up too soon.
You leaned on your stick just feet from your ancestor.

The clods flew, I knelt to copy down
the rest of the inscription as it emerged,
Joyce clicked her camera; the sunlight was on us all.
These were the glories of Burton Dassett.

Spuggies

The spuggies are back –
a word I lifted from Basil Bunting
and was never entirely sure how to pronounce,
having only seen it in print, in *Briggflatts*,
and at the time had little cause to adopt
with the London sparrow in extinction;
but now three are cheeping in my lilacs.

The other word I learned from Basil Bunting
he spoke aloud, the last time I met him:
'bleb', meaning condom – as used, he said
(to his severe disapprobation)
by 12-year-old girls on the Tyne & Wear
housing estate where we were calling on him.
I think they asked him if he had any.

Fox

Our old fox creaks into the garden,
a rusty shadow. He finds a patch of sun,
curls up for ten minutes; dozes.

Then suddenly he's bounding into the air,
leaping on imaginary frogs in the periwinkle
and snatching intently at the lawn.

What can he be chewing in his long, long jaws?
I peer from the bedroom through binoculars.
Grass. I shall never understand him.

The Saucer

Round here I saw a flying saucer once
on a sultry night like this: July, still light.
I was walking with my gaze fixed on the moon
over the rooftops when it loomed: the classic

flattened dome, almost a cartoon version.
I tracked it all along Fortis Green,
to the High Road. No one else seemed to see it;
normal people don't look up at the sky.

I marched after it among dawdling couples.
A man came out of the chip shop, munching;
I was tempted to clutch him as a witness –
but you don't, do you? And it moved so fast,

scooting low to the south over Highgate,
then out of sight. An advertising gimmick,
I told myself: a motorised balloon,
some kind of airship; not worth mentioning.

But now I think of the disappointed creatures,
wistful in their skyborne chapter house,
as they chugged back to the mother planet
taking whatever they had brought for us.

The Belly Dancer

Across the road the decorators have finished;
your flat has net curtains again
after all these weeks, and a 'To Let' sign.

I can only think of it as a tomb,
excavated, in the end, by
explorers in facemasks and protective spacesuits.

No papers, no bank account, no next of kin;
only a barricade against the landlord,
and the police at our doors, early, with questions.

What did we know? Not much: a Lebanese name,
a soft English voice; chats in the street
in your confiding phase; the dancing.

You sat behind me once at midnight Mass.
You were Orthodox, really; church
made you think of your mother, and cry.

From belly dancer to recluse, the years
and the stealthy ballooning of your outline,
kilo by kilo, abducted you.

Poor girl, I keep saying; poor girl –
no girl, but young enough to be my daughter.
I called at your building once, canvassing;

your face loomed in the hallway and, forgetting
whether or not we were social kissers,
I bounced my lips on it. It seemed we were not.

They've even replaced your window frames. I still
imagine a midden of flesh, and that smell
you read about in reports of earthquakes.

They say there was a heart beside your doorbell
upstairs. They say all sorts. They would –
who's to argue? I don't regret the kiss.

Ingeburg

Putting it in a poem is no use,
but she won't see it on the internet
(she's blind) or hear it on the radio,
drawn to her attention by some friend –
last time we spoke she had none; even
her late husband's boring niece had died.

An old, blind, bad-tempered, scholarly
Jewish widow with a German accent,
half-paralysed, stuck in a born-again
Christian care home in small-town Canada.

Except that now she's gone. No, not dead, and
no, they couldn't tell me any more.

No doubt they thought I was after her money.

*

Exactly how was she so irritating?
Being bossy (well, she was a teacher);
befriending and pestering my parents;
interfering; forcing me (thank God)
to study Greek.
                    But mostly it was that
I didn't care for being doted on.

Not just 'the best student she'd ever had'
but my 'funny little nose pressed against
the windowpane' that day we spilt the ink,
Diane and I, on her front room carpet
while she was out. The flat stank for weeks
of the milk we sloshed on so it wouldn't stain.

Fancy forgiving me for that!

Of course she scored points with us for her 'secret'
affair with a married professor; we found
the hypocrisy most entertaining.
(My father knew him; he spoke at my wedding.)
And after a while we all moved on,
she and I to live in different countries.

*

I've not spoken to her for eighteen months.
What would I want, if I could track her down?
To know she's all right – or whatever
constitutes being 'all right' for someone
of ninety-four, other than being dead,
which in her state of health would be my choice.

I'd like to hear her voice. I'd like to know
if there's anything I can send her.
I'd like to apologise.

I'd quite like to be forgiven again.

Alfred

(i.m. Alfred Robinson, 1861-1934)

Suddenly I've outlived my grandfather:
the one for whom I was unique, his only
grandchild, although eleven more were to come.

An infant bundle on his bedside rug,
I must have heard the not yet fathomable
murmurs of his farewell to my mother.

'Tell her about me when she's older,' he said.
She did better than that: she gave me
his complete Shakespeare, 1928,

bought the year after, on Shakespeare's birthday –
just the kind of thing I might have done.
The print is tiny, to my ageing eyes.

Thirty-seven plays, in eight-point type.
I read them in my teens, lying on the carpet
in my bedroom, and ticking them off as I went:

Hamlet (tick), *Macbeth* (tick), *Henry the Fifth* (tick) –
goodbye, Grandpa – *The Tempest* (tick) – thank you –
and the sonnets, of course; and *Romeo*...

Match Girl

She grew up, the little match girl;
leapfrogged a century, survived,
became my little sister: small-boned
and slender still, but breakable.

When she had measles I was there;
I remember her chickenpox,
her whooping cough, her grumbling appendix,
and when she ran into the barbed wire.

But how can someone younger than me
have osteoporosis, and sit
googling up a substance that might
help it, or give her phossy jaw?

Phosphorus. It can strengthen brittle
bones – or turn them into rubble.

Alumnae Notes

Beautiful Ataneta Swainson is dead.
I had a crush on her when she was a prefect
(hers is the face that swims into my head

when Katherine Mansfield's Maata is mentioned);
and Barbara Murray, my fellow cyclist
and fan of Rupert Brooke, has dementia.

The class photos fade. But Marie and I,
face to face on Skype in full colour
and still far too animated to die,

can see we've not yet turned to sepia.

Nominal Aphasia

On the bus, 'mirage' was waiting for me.
I had left it there on my way out, dodging
under the seats, refusing to be collared,

lurking among 'deception' and 'illusion'
and 'fantasy' and 'phantom' and, I confess,
'oasis' (you can see the logic there).

It was in a dim, swimming, sandy turmoil
of desert vistas. I couldn't even get
that it might begin with 'm', or be French.

But the minute I stepped aboard, going home,
the word skipped briskly into my head,
impatient at having been kept waiting.

Walking Stick

Parading on the pharmacy carpet
as I try out the height, I'm taken back
to the time I bought my first high heels
(brown suede, with little bows, if you must know);
walking with something new is a knack.

I can still see Grandma Adcock's pursed lips.
'Never mind,' whispered Mother; 'once in a while
it's nice to buy something your grandmother
disapproves of.' Well, this respectable
piece of apparatus is just her style.

'It's only temporary,' I say – 'a sprain –
you know these rough pavements – I had a fall.'
Yes, temporary this time. But who's fooled?
The stick's a folding one, in a plastic case.
I'll keep it hanging ready in the hall.

Macular Degeneration

For a start, I'm fairly sure they're not swans:
too many (this is not Coole Park),
although flapping such wide white underwings.
Also too squat. Are they geese, perhaps?
If I could work out the scale; if they were
closer... Or what about seagulls?

All this restless taking off and landing
doesn't help; it's a very broad pond –
more a lake – and they're on the other side.
I need something to measure them against:
that moorhen, for example, bumbling around
(these glasses are useless) – unless it's a coot?

Now they're off again, wheeling and swooping,
waterskiing. If only they would
kindly stop all this buggering about
and proceed calmly in my direction.
The light's not too good for judging colours.
Settle down, damn you! I think they're ducks.

Mrs Baldwin

And then there's the one about the old woman
who very apologetically asks the way
to Church Lane, adding 'I ought to know:
I've lived there since the war.' So you go with her.

This comes with variations, usually leading
(via a list of demented ancestors)
to calculations of how much time you've got
before you're asking the way to your own house.

But it's not so often that you find the one
about how, whenever you hear of someone
diagnosed with cancer, you have to hide
that muffled pang that clutched you, at fifteen,
when you saw Pauline Edwards holding hands
with the boy from the Social Club you'd always fancied.

Charon

Where is Dr Shipman when we need him
to ferry us across the fatal stream
and land us gently in Elysium?

Shipman, boatman, ferryman – whatever
the craft he plies to help us cross the river –
we seem to have been waiting here for ever.

How did we get the timetable so wrong?
Things are becoming vague, and we're not strong.
Life was OK, but it went on too long.

When we've forgotten how to keep afloat,
scoop us up, Doctor, in your kindly boat,
and carry us across the final moat.

Having Sex with the Dead

How can it be reprehensible?
The looks on their dead faces, as they plunge
into you, your hand circling a column

of one-time flesh and pulsing blood that now
has long been ash and dispersed chemicals.
The half-glimpsed mirror over their shoulders.

This one on the floor of his sitting-room
unexpectedly, one far afternoon;
that one whose house you broke into, climbing

through his bathroom window after a row.
The one who called you a mermaid; the one
who was gay, really, but you both forgot.

They have all forgotten now: forgotten
you and their wives and the other mermaids
who slithered in their beds and took their breath.

Disentangle your fingers from their hair.
Let them float away, like Hylas after
the nymphs dragged him gurgling into the pool.

TESTATORS

Robert Harington, 1558

Get you, with your almain rivetts (latest
fad from Germany), and your corselet,
and your two coats of plate! How much harness

does a man need? None, when he's in his grave.
Your sons may have it, together with your
damask and satin gowns to show off in;

while you go to lie down in Witham church,
and the most armour I've seen in a will
rusts or turns ridiculous in this world.

Anthony Cave, 1558

One monument to her dear Antony
was not enough. Even his will allowed for
two: 'no sumptuous pomp,' he said, but
a stone 'of no great value' in the north aisle

and 'a picture of death upon the wall.'
It hovers above him, engraved in brass,
a skeleton trussed in a transparent shroud
like a polythene bag: '*So shall you be.*'

Elizabeth, who would have cradled his bones,
saw all done; and then, as she must,
married twice more – Chicheley was a prize.
Eighteen years later, widowed a third time,

her four daughters dowried and settled,
and the future of the house secure,
she was Anthony's again; and yielded
to a degree of sumptuous pomp.

This is the third monument: of marble –
with caryatids, I'm afraid, and columns.
In front lies a naked corpse, hands clasped
modestly over its parts; above this

a row of kneeling figures – short-lived son
behind him, train of daughters behind her –
and they two, face to face across a desk,
gazing and gazing at each other.

Alice Adcock, 1673

Sitting by the widow's bed, the vicar
made notes: to her sons and her daughter
£2 apiece; to every grandchild
five shillings; her bed and bedding; a chest...

Then it began to be all petticoats:
to her daughter, 'my jersey petticoat';
'my petticoat and my hat' (to a friend);
'my green petticoat and the body of

my jersey gown' (to her son Robert's wife);
'my tawny coat' (to her son William);
and (to his wife) 'my ordinary wearing
petticoat and the coat I wear under it.'

Even allowing for the fact
that a petticoat was merely a skirt
and not underwear, this is confusing:
what, in the context, was a coat?

The vicar dutifully wrote it up.
But her brother-in-law, named executor,
flinched from allocating such tricky
female garments and renounced the task.

Instead her son Robert shouldered it –
as he did that of generating,
in their eventual multitudes,
all the subsequent Adcocks in Syston.

Luke Sharpe, 1704

'I, Luke Sharpe of Langham, desiring
that all my children may live together
in peace and love... do make
this my last will and testament.

To my daughters one hundred pounds apiece...
my son Luke Sharpe my executor...'
and then a growl from the beyond: 'My will
notwithstanding the above is that

if my daughter Elizabeth Sharpe
be married to Mr Kempe of Oakham
or any other man without consent
and liking of my executor

she shall have but one shilling for her portion.'
The same goes for Mary, vis-à-vis
Thomas Bodell (not even '*Mr*' Bodell).
I'd like to think she ran away with him.

As for Elizabeth, she knuckled under,
let her brother talk her into a match
with Mr William Lacer of Syston
(she was past thirty); became an ancestor.

William Clayton, 1725

'I give and bequeath to my beloved son
John Clayton all my tools
proper for the trade of a carpenter' –
this among careful provisions
for his two daughters and their families:
a cottage that he's lately rebuilt,
a rood of land each in the common field.

Twenty-three years later, the will
of John Clayton of Syston, carpenter –
half the length, and more perfunctory,
with all that he owns left to his wife, and
after her death to a list of daughters:
Mary, wife of William Adcock,
Elizabeth, wife of John Taylor,
Ann, Katherine, Hannah, Sarah and Jane
Clayton – the seven survivors
of nine female births in a row
uninterrupted by anything male.

No carpentry tools are mentioned.

James Heyes, 1726

To be a prizer is a solemn task –
to value all his Goods, Cattells and Chattells
for a *True and perfect Inventory*,
the stock first: *Two old Cows and two Calves,*
£6 5s, one old Horse, one Colt...
assessing his crops – *Wheat and Barley*
upon the ground £8; Oats 5 shillings;
Pottatoes £1.10s (good soil
for root crops now they've drained part of the Mere
around Burscough); *A few garden pulse –*

then his cart and husbandry implements;
and in the house the *Grate & Crow & Tongues,*
the *Rakins and other Iron Geere,*
his *Two Small old brass pans,* his *One brass pott,*
All the Pewter (no need to count it);
his diverse tubs and vessels: *One Eshin,*
One Piggin (let the clerk spell them), *One*
Salting Turnall, One Washing Turnall,
One Stoond (for beer); *One Tresl; Four old Chears;*
One fall board; One Table & the Forme...

We recognise these things; we have their like
in our own houses; his *Old Fether bed*
with its Furnature might be one of ours.
We have apprised his every item,
even to the *old Grindle Stone* (sixpence),
but the total, just over £30,
is £4 short of the poor fellow's debts –
and his eldest lad barely come of age,
with three young sisters... Well, here is our list,
duly signed. *William Foreshaw. William Prescot.*

Henry Eggington, 1912

'I want no funeral service
in any shape whatsoever...'

It may not have been what Eva
expected of her father's will:

'I instruct my executors
(Eva and her brother Thomas)

to have my body cremated
as soon as possible. No flowers

nor black to be worn but simply
taken to the Withington Road

crematorium, and the ashes
scattered to the four winds of the earth.'

                                             *

'And that no person follow my
remains but the executors.'

Eva may have disobeyed him –
she and Nellie were photographed

in black dresses about this time
(unless that was for Marion,

recently dead at twenty-four).
But to follow her father's coffin

I hope she had a winter coat
in dutiful grey, brown or blue,

for a January morning
in Manchester; or a warm shawl.

                                             *

'No one to attend the reading
of my will but those interested' –

that is to say, mentioned in it:
his wife, of course; Thomas, Eva,

James, Nellie, Harry. Not Mary
(who was married to a scoundrel

and far too fond of money herself)
or Willie (what had Willie done?)

The rest set out, obediently
disguised as non-mourners, hoping

their nervous mufti would provoke
no reaction from the neighbours.

                                        *

To have TB at sixty, caught
from nursing a daughter till she died,

and to hear another daughter
(the pet, the youngest) and a son

already coughing the same cough
can sicken a man of playing,

as he once did, Moody and Sankey's
jolly hymns on the harmonium.

Nellie and James would both be dead
within three years (and Willie, too –

of something quite unsuspected).
Meanwhile those who had to do it

incinerated Henry's beard,
his rotten lungs, his broken heart,

his anger, and cast them to the four winds.

William Dick Mackley

For 'general dealer' read 'fence': he served
a year in Warwick jail for receiving
'12 tame fowls, feloniously stolen'.
Arrogant enough to plead not guilty,
he went down for twice as long as the thief.

But yes, he was a general dealer too,
with his scrapyard in Catherine Street
full of everything, or pieces of it –
an embarrassment, no doubt, to Rosetta's
more genteel cousins if they should pass by.

No doubt? But the whole thing rattles with doubts:
was he really, for example, a Gypsy,
or just a besotted hanger-on who
travelled with fairground people, dodged the census
as often as not; lived in a caravan?

Ah, that Diccon-the-Gypsy glamour! Of course
Rosetta fell: married him in Leicester,
seven months pregnant; hawked fish in Swindon
under a false name; buried dead infants
along the way to wherever might be next.

For twenty years the shadows engulf them –
drifting, disguised. Then in 1901
they trundle into town with the funfair –
Ada Ann, their only surviving child,
is a 'travelling shooting gallery'.

Ten years later William is breaking stones,
with Rosetta left in charge of the business,
an entry in the Leicester directory –
The Van, Catherine Street – and her will made
(decades too early). I seem to see her

in shawl and braids on the steps of the van,
smoking a pipe on a summer evening.
(I try to obliterate the pipe; no,
it won't go). But she died in a 'rest home',
smashed up falling from a bedroom window.

William inherited £2,000
(solid money from her solid father?)
and left nearly twice that to his new wife.
Not exactly a Gypsy thing, a will.
And how did Rosetta fall out of the window?

The Translator

(in memory of my ancestor Robert Tighe, d.1616)

I

Anne Browne's grandfather, he turned out to be.
No wonder she bequeathed books in her will:
'Charnocks sermons upon the attributes
and Doctor Burnetts church history' – these
to a son-in-law; then *'Item I give*
to my daughter Hurst my Cambridge Bible.'

That Bible might have been a clue; first, though,
where was she from: Kirby? Careby? Some small
Danelaw village near the Rutland border
in Lincolnshire. They all sounded the same
to the vicar of St Mary Woolnoth
in London when he married her parents.

But two years later, 1631,
in the register at Carlby, *'Anne Tigh*
daughter to John Tigh baptised June vij'.
John was swallowed up in the Civil War;
during which same commotion Anne married
Samuel Browne of Stockinghall, Rutland.

Carlby, then. But the register patchy,
no earlier Tighe entries, John's mother
buried as her second husband's widow
'Marie Bawtrie' (to be unmasked later).
So who was her first? The Lay Subsidy
returns, for the land tax, surrendered him:

in the 8th regnal year of James I,
'[...] Tyghe doctor in Divinity' – first name
obliterated. It doesn't matter;
there was only going to be one match.
The Oxford and Cambridge alumni lists
rolled out his multiple identities:

'Tighe, Robert, of Deeping, Lincs. BA from
Trinity College, Cambridge. BD and
DD, Magdalen College, Oxford. Vicar
of All Hallows' (from whose tower Pepys would
view the fire). *'Archdeacon of Middlesex.*
One of the translators of the Bible.'

II

Being him:
sifting through flakes and flecks
of Hebrew; winnowing out
seeds of meaning; choking
on obscurities, the chaff
of mistranscriptions, howlers,
ambiguities, the never-before-seen.

Dreaming it:
the braids of upside-down-looking
words trailing through his sleep,
tripping him up or winding themselves
into suddenly obvious patterns:
truth leaping out;
no room for argument.

But arguing anyway:
someone, Tyndale or whoever,
may have got it wrong –
just this one term,
perhaps, for a beast or a tree;
an odd verb; a tribal name;
a turn of phrase that needed to be recast.

III

After all, they had chosen him for it:
celeberrimus textuarius –
the lad from a dull yeoman family
in Deeping St James, who went to Cambridge
and grew into a 'profound linguist'
(as Fuller has it) – rose to his moment.

After his doctorate, after he left
scholastic seclusion to get an heir,
found a wife and a parish, began to
baptise his own children (most of whom died),
and stuffed the graveyard with plague burials
while the new Scottish King quaked and delayed,

came the call: to join the First Westminster
Company under Lancelot Andrewes
and re-examine an allotted chunk
of the Old Testament. Andrewes himself
took the Pentateuch, with a few yes-men;
Tighe and his fellows broached the histories.

Elsewhere, companies of learned divines
combed their way through the Hebrew and Greek texts
of the remaining Scriptures (without pay –
their other duties had to support them)
for some five years: conferring, reviewing,
meeting again, squabbling for perfection.

Selden relates how they went about it:
one reading, the others interrupting
to correct any fault. It was all done
by voice, testing it on the ear for sense
and euphony. Almost no one took notes.
The great process lies buried in hearsay.

IV

And Robert? No sooner excavated
from the silt of documentary darkness
than he slithers away again: a black gown
among other such around a table,
offering suggestions when the urge impels him
but not, it seems, writing anything down.

We have his signature as vicar
on page after page of the register
at All Hallows; but otherwise
no identifiable word of his:
no letters, no books or sermons,
even his will declared invalid and lost.

He has merged into a composite –
we can make contact with that mind
only in his assent, grudged or willing,
quite often tacit, no doubt,
as the procedural rules enjoined,
to Joshua, Judges, Ruth, Samuel, the books of Kings.

Intestate

What was she supposed to use for ink –
blood? Breast milk? Amniotic fluid?

Too late for those. Too late altogether.
Some things are impossible to write.

CAMPBELLS

Elegy for Alistair

(i.m. Alistair Te Ariki Campbell, 1925-2009)

Now he is dead, who wrote
'Now he is dead, who talked
of wild places and skies
inhabited by the hawk' –

thereby captivating
readers and composers,
envious fellow-poets,
multiple admirers

of his romantic looks,
and silly girls like me,
foolish enough to marry
what I wanted to be

before I knew who I was
but wise enough to have chosen
a kind and dedicated
father for our children

who happened as well to have
an exquisite ear and eye
for a rhythm or a phrase.
Beautiful poet, goodbye.

Port Charles

It must have been August. I was nineteen.
My husband and I and our friend John Thomson

hitchhiked for hours, pole-axed by Marzine,
on sick-making bends to that far bay.

The bach was a rustic hut in the bush:
bellbirds by day, and by night moreporks

and an atmospheric trek with a torch
through ferny rustles to the outside dunny.

Alistair pretended to be joking
when he quailed and shuddered; but no: it seemed

we couldn't tease him back into reason.
I had married a man who suffered from ghosts.

He had been a child in the haunted islands
where his parents were buried. Too much darkness.

For me, though, the prevailing spirit
was of something beginning to dawn.

I was prospectively possessed by
the phantom of the yet-to-be-born:

an inconceivable, newly conceived
co-presence, visible so far only

as a coded smudge under my eyes.
Who says you can't be 'slightly pregnant'?

What the 1950s Were Like

As if you'd scarcely even noticed
the lavatory was across the yard
in the wash-house, and you all had to go
outside, day or night, raining or not,
pregnant or not, for every pee;

and since your mother had never told you
tipping in Harpic was not enough,
the lodger had to speak out, fed up
with her teenage landlady, who'd never
learnt to use a lavatory brush.

Student life was one state (Miss Gillon
ruling over her warren of arty youths
at 191 The Terrace), living at home
another. This was a third condition:
student marriage, it could have been called.

Clues: the Festival of Britain curtains,
the record-player, the new LPs,
the no TV (this was New Zealand);
and, with luck, Bohemian role models
calling in on the way home from the pub.

The Royal Visit

I took my baby to see the Queen.
He was not yet born, but she wouldn't wait.
She was wearing an evening gown
of silver brocade, although it was lunchtime;
but then she was opening Parliament.

I had on a maternity smock –
it wasn't the thing to parade your bulge,
even for a respectable woman
like me, married more than a year.
Pregnancy was a little bit rude.

It took five minutes from my house,
facing the bulk of Tinakori Hill,
to Parliament and the sunshiny crowds.
I didn't wave, but the baby inside me
waggled his limbs in a loyal kick.

S.S. Gothic was chugging south
around the coastline to scoop up the Queen
from Bluff on a date long preordained.
Meanwhile biology and hormones
were organising my own rendezvous.

Two months later, when I'd turned twenty
and given birth, I'd find myself chanting
'I've got a B.A. and a B.A.B.Y.'
I could almost believe my life would glide on
with the smoothly oiled timing of a royal tour.

The Professor of Music

Standing behind me at the counter
of that old general store in Molesworth Street
where the National Library now looms,

Freddie Page remarked of my purchases –
a tin of black pepper and a mousetrap –
'What a surrealistic pair of objects!'

Later, on a rare visit to our house,
he teased us for having acquired a fridge.
Could we be getting above ourselves?

But ever since the time when a small maggot
had trekked across the plate of a guest
at our table, from a slice of cold lamb,

I couldn't quite trust our meat-safe;
and we had a young child now; and also
my sister had an opulent Frigidaire.

Coconut Matting

Trying to save our marriage, my parents
laid linoleum over the matting
I'd stitched seam by seam with a curved needle,

and glued fake Formica on my deal table
for a surprise when we came back.
Sterile beige smothered our living-room.

How could they get it so wrong? And how could we
tell them? We muttered some nothings,
and slunk away in different directions.

Let's rush up to heaven right now and cling together,
all of us, in a huddle of sobs,
apologising and forgiving each other.

Epithalamium

(for Gregory's wedding to Angela, Wellington, 8 December 2007)

Jetlagged again, I greet my precious firstborn
through the usual haze of 'Am I still awake?'

Our ups and downs, through half a century,
could be described as aeronautical:

though you're the qualified pilot, I'm the one
who, far too often, flew away from you.

Well, here I am again, for yet another
rediscovery of my grown-up son.

Remember when we tootled off as tourists
to the South Island (early '76)?

First the flight to Dunedin (still a treat
for a struggling student – 'All you need is money',

you said in wonderment); then the hire car
(I paid, you drove), and off to Central Otago

through landscapes where I'd hitchhiked with your father
a quarter of a century before.

Tracking memories, we constructed more –
I'm thinking of that pub in Alexandra

where the pianist, who turned out to be psychic,
struck up 'Careless Love' before we could ask.

Now you and Angela take off together
in love that's neither flyaway nor careless.

All the best for the future, then, my darlings.
Bon voyage, and many happy landings.

A Novelty

(for my great-grandson Seth Lucas Campbell, born 19 November 2011)

What was the bun they had in the oven?
Another girl for my charm bracelet
of granddaughters and great-granddaughters?
Or a male of the species, crested not cloven:
a son, a lad, a fellow, a fella,
heir to the family name, a princelet,
a chap, a bloke, a joker, a geezer,
a guy, a man-child, a mister, a master,
a chip off the old block for his father,
a grandson for Gregory, a joy
for his grandmothers in their several degrees
to cherish, a new kind of cuddly toy
for his aunts and little cousins to squeeze?
Yes! Ollie and Kirsty have had a boy.

MY LIFE WITH ARTHROPODS

Wet Feet

I was up to my knees in the slit trench
alongside the common, after tadpoles,
when a miniature crocodile bit my leg.

I exaggerate, of course; it nibbled.
I snatched it off, saw what was in my hand,
and flung it back in the water: a monster.

Much later I learned its romantic name:
damsel-fly nymph – a fit inhabitant,
by the sound of it, for my fairy poems.

Meanwhile my sister and I, fossicking
in the ditch at the end of our garden,
found what some kids told us were caddis-flies:

tiny cylindrical clumps of debris –
leaf litter, chopped stalks, diminutive stones –
that would creep nervously across your hand.

They were grubs, really, naked inside their
cunningly decorated sleeping-bags.
You wouldn't have wanted to undress one.

That the wet and squidgy was a kingdom
of shape-shifters, where anything you found
might have plans to turn into something else,

came as a part of the portfolio
handed from child to child, together with
where best to go scrumping, and the local

version of Eeny-meeny-macka-racka.

Dung Beetle

Not easy to forget, the 'sacred beetle' –
excavator, scavenger, hoarder
of what we all want to be rid of –
a creature, I have to confess,
I've never set eyes on, but read about
indelibly in *The Insect Man*:

it burrowed into my nine-year-old mind,
head down, walking backwards, hind legs
rolling a great ball of shit and instinct
and science wrapped up holus-bolus
for me to store in my own underground
larder and feed on, like a beetle's child.

Caterpillars

In the last August of the war, my
caterpillars died of starvation:
all of them, large or small, green or striped,
the hawk moth one with his spiky tail,
the long floppy ones off the poplar,
the black woolly bear, my favourite
(I kidded myself that he'd escaped).

We'd gone on holiday to Ireland.
I had asked Derek, the boy upstairs,
to feed them. He had full instructions.
He was twelve, a year older than me;
he had seemed all right.
                          But how could I
have entrusted my helpless infants –
sealed in their shoe boxes and jam jars,
each with the right leaves, and totally
reliant on me for fresh supplies –
to a boy, even if he promised?
A boy, no matter which one? A boy.

Stag Beetle

'Dead Baby Stag Beetle' reads the caption
in my illustrated nature diary.
Other pages have 'Bee on Hollyhock
(from life)', 'Fungus (from life)'. The beetle sketch
is pedantically subtitled not

'from death' (too histrionic, did I think?)
but 'from the real one'. More reality
or more biology would have told me
that this was just any dead black beetle;
a juvenile stag beetle is a grub.

If I'd been introduced to one, and known
its future (a small black Spitfire, whirring
through the dusk to clash in armoured battle
over its mate), the scientist in me
would no doubt still have contrived to be charmed.

Praying Mantis

Green as a leek, this unlikely insect
is squatting on Grandma's flowering hedge
in dragon pose, but with long arms folded
under its triangular head, to pounce.

We had to ask its name; no one told us
about mantises – mantids? Mantidae? –
how can you relate to a creature that
doesn't even have a proper plural?

Are they new here, like us? I remember
the house and garden from when I was five,
but not these coloured paper cutouts, poised
silently on unusual foliage.

Grandma and our parents have things to do.
We drift around the orchard, gossiping
about life on the boat – our favourite
stewards; those lavatories in Panama.

Then back to nature study. Why am I
reminded of the Wizard of Oz, when
Jiminy Cricket is more to the point?
We seem to be living in a cartoon.

Flea

One excellent quality of the flea
is its capacity to embarrass,
for example, the wealthy art dealer
who kindly drove you and two of your friends
from Dorset to London, but who wouldn't
acknowledge what you'd caught in his back seat;
his discomfiture will be repeated
until he stops being in denial
and takes the car to be fumigated.

Another pleasure is the fatal crunch
when you compress one between two thumbnails.

Then there's the fun of seeing how they hop
shamelessly from one host to another –
as on the train when a flea you've acquired
by visiting a cat-owning household
jumps from your sleeve to the one beside you.
It seems too late for an apology;
better to pretend you haven't noticed.

The first I ever met were chicken fleas
caught from playing in an empty henhouse;
peering down the front of my vest, I could
watch them scurry off under my armpits.
Auntie's reaction was gratifying.

My own reaction was allergic.

Hoppy

Found on the hillside above Urbino:
a grasshopper missing one long leg,
instantly named by eight-year-old Andrew
and almost as swiftly immortalised
by my camera, once I was back from
running down to our *pensione* for it;
during which time he had sat raptly guarding
the small shadow you can still see on his hand:

the tenderness of the future vet, perhaps –
who dropped out, having mistaken his calling;
the future anthropologist, musician,
publisher and family man; the kind child
who was to reveal, as perhaps even then
I should have been able to prophesy,
that of all the gifts blossoming in him
his supreme talent is for fatherhood.

To the Mosquitoes of Auckland

(on discovering that I am not allergic to them).

Come, then, mosquitoes of my youth:
feel free to munch me with impunity.
Your forebears, nibbling at my infant flesh,
blessed me with permanent immunity.

Stick Insects

Sweeping the kitchen floor I scooped up
in the dustpan an angular wiry tangle –
part of my grandchildren's construction kit?
(This was their house.) A clutter of dead twigs?
Some kind of three-dimensional puzzle?
That, certainly: a pair of stick insects
locked in complicated sexual congress.

Phasmids. Phasmatidae. Lives devoted to
being something else; relying on dignity,
for want of speed – standing around looking
vegetal, ligneous or metallic.
Once I saw one stalking across a road
by the Botanical Gardens, caught out
behaving for a change like flesh and blood.

These two had risked invading a house
(she the explorer, he clinging piggyback)
until my broom scuttled them. They seemed unhurt
and not at all inclined to disengage.
That part of Karori is green with bush.
I carried them respectfully on the dustpan,
still in their embrace, to a matching tree.

Crayfish

Of course with all those legs they're arthropods –
crayfish, lobsters and their armoured ilk.
At school one day a bunch of us nipped out
in our lunch-break and bought a prickly hulk
to have our way with, rip apart and crunch.

It was like eating a pterodactyl –
morally, I mean, in retrospect –
but the sea-drenched jelly when I snapped
a leg from the carapace, cracked it and sucked in
ecstasy...no, that's no way to talk.

Think of the blood-orange-pink smashed shards,
the pimpled plates of the exoskeleton,
reduced to midden-debris, wrapped
in newspaper in the prefects' room bin;
think of the handsome creature; feel the guilt.

Archaic, slow to mature, not adult
for ten years, it lurks deep among rocks:
the spiny or rock lobster – the one that lacks
claws. To shock predators when attacked
it screeches with its quavering antennae:

friction, not vocalisation. Moult by moult,
given time, it can grow to the bulk
of a dog. Cilla McQueen said it can walk
all the way across the bed of the Tasman
to Australia, feeler to feeler with its kin.

Slaters

The English woodlouse doesn't curl up
into a neat ball when you touch it
like the slater of my childhood
(your pill bug or roly-poly, perhaps).

It seems a missed opportunity
to introduce more entertainment
into the garden; so thank God
for that other multi-nominal

dome-shaped creature, the ladybird
(ladybug, lady cow, if you wish) –
gloss-coloured, with counting-lesson spots
and its own personal nursery rhyme –

commemorated in my house
by the fridge-magnet Cait left behind
(but has since told me I may keep),
lost under the sofa when she was three.

Ella's Crane-flies

Dear Ella, this is a gentle plea
for the daddy-longlegs population
that haunts your room. Don't hoover them up:
let me convert you to conservation.

A dozen years ago I might
have told you they were fairies in disguise,
but now that you're of age I'll say
try seeing them as skinny butterflies.

No? It was never going to work;
phobias aren't susceptible to words.
You'll never love the leggy wisps.
But think of the planet; think of the birds.

Insects are edible, even these
fragile flitters in their gossamer dance.
Let them be hunted; shoo them out
through the open windows to take their chance.

Orb Web

My tiger flashing stripy legs
up and down the geometry
suspended in my pantry window,
scurrying over cleats and crossings

or twinkletoes across a guy-rope
to sniff with diagnostic feet
at whatever she may have trapped
in her tensile architecture,

can't comprehend the role of 'pet'
which I try to impose on her
by fending off arachnophobes
and hurling greenfly into her net –

all very sweet if the present tense
were not in this case historic,
referring ('wistfully') to an autumn
back in the decade before last

when half the garden was out of bounds,
zigzagged with no-go filaments,
the omphalos of every web
studded with a hirsute acorn

squatting plumply in the ether;
I had to deflect the window-cleaner
from the front of the house, to save
luscious danglers draped on the panes.

These days the only ones we harbour
are floor-scuttlers with no charisma
or miniatures, indulged in corners,
trawling for midges with formless wisps.

Come back, defectors: find your way
from brambles in secluded thickets;
come, furry-trousered velvet raisins,
come and bedizen my house again!

My Grubby Little Secret

Under armchairs, inside the carpet:
rows of miniature white papooses

in which, when I tugged an occupant,
it stretched into a prehensile thread.

All the chemicals that work are banned;
there was only the vacuum-cleaner,

with its cruel attachments, to mince,
grind and suck up the little victims

together with their woolly foodstuff
into a sickening fluffy mash.

But no one looks under furniture;
I had only to stay in control,

slaughtering on the quiet – until
I found two new nurseries, thriving.

That was it. I'd have the lot stripped out;
enough of this maggoty lifestyle.

I ordered an invented fibre
no moth would touch. There was just the shame...

but the carpet fitters were as cool
as a proctology clinic nurse

viewing yet another shy bottom;
they knew half the houses in my street.

In Provence

You know you're not in England when
at siesta time you open
what seemed a sealed pack of biscuits,
take an unguarded bite, and find
you're being bitten in return.

A rush to the bathroom mirror
reveals a sketchy black moustache
inscribed along your upper lip:
the smallest ants you've ever seen,
hotly exacting their revenge.

Well, what did you expect? Vineyards
and lavender-fields accoutred
with nothing more aggressive than
a limelight-hogging swallowtail?
Ants are the maquis. Blame the sun.

Unmentionable

'Crab lice, author's experience of'
is an index entry you won't find
in my not-to-be-written memoirs,

although I could tell a tale or two
about the man who gave them to me
(he left them out of his own such books),

and the far too curious GP
who saw my predicament as a
personal invitation to him;

not to mention my naive young friend,
wearing a woolly hat in summer,
who told us he'd caught some from his wife,

who told him she'd caught them (oh, really?)
from her social work with the homeless.
But in fact I think those were head lice.

Phobia

My little sister fell off a dry-stone wall
when a wasp flew down the back of her dress.

That same summer in Wiltshire, our mother
turned over some pears in a greengrocer's

and suddenly lay down on the floor.
An allergic family; so what of me,

whose face a mere Venetian mosquito
could turn into the Elephant Man's?

For decades I quailed, but was never stung.
I read about anaphylactic shock –

how Susan Hill, barefoot in her bedroom,
stepped on a tiny corpse and nearly died;

how a wasp on his ice cream killed a child.
Would my own death zing in yellow stripes?

It seemed I was destined not to find out,
until one August in a leafy alley

something explosive shot under my hat
and stabbed my forehead just at the hairline.

Nothing happened. I didn't faint, or choke,
or feel ill; what I felt was exultant.

I soared above the pavements all the way
to a pharmacy (for antihistamine,

just in case), barely resisting the urge
to babble like an earthquake survivor.

Blowflies

If you liked them, how your heart might have lifted
to see their neat trapezium shapes studding
the wall like a newly landed flight of jet
ornaments, the intensity of their black
gloss, with secret blues and greens half-glinting through,
and the glass wings, not so unlike those of bees –

if you could bring yourself; if they occupied
a niche in creation nudged fractionally
sideways –
                because it's not their present forms, it's
their larval incarnations that you can't stop
heaving into view, white nests moistly seething
in a dead pigeon or a newspaper-wrapped
package leaking beside a path (but enough –
the others will kindly absent themselves, please!)

And wondering what, where – under the floorboards
or behind the freezer – suddenly hatched these.

Bat Soup

But it's diluted with sky, not water,
the aerial plankton on which they sup.
Our solitary pipistrelle flickers
over her chosen suburban quarter,
echo-locating, to siphon it up.
It nourishes birds as well as bats –
high-flyers that feed on the wing,
swifts, house-martins – this floating gruel
of hymenoptera, midges and gnats,
thunderbugs, beetles, aphids, flies,
moths, mosquitoes, and flying dots
almost too small to be worth naming.

Some of it swirls at a lower level –
a broth of midges over a pool
at dusk or a simultaneous hatch
of mayflies boiling up from Lough Neagh:
swallow-fodder, and also a splotch
to plaster on any passing windscreen,
though even at speed there's never so much
as of yore; bad news for the food-chain,
but somehow *'ou sont les neiges d'antan'*
sounds too noble a note of dole
for a sullying mash of blood and chitin.
(And we can't hear what the bats are screaming).

Lepidoptera

Before there were butterflies, there was a moth
cupped in my mother's palm for me to stroke
and not be frightened. I remember no fear:
only soft brown fur under my finger.

*

Such light walkers, with such delicate legs
to support the ornate curtains of their wings.
But that's why they need the air to waft in –
and ours they find less wholesome year by year.

Long past summers were frilly with butterflies.
I could stare down from my bathroom window
at peacocks, red admirals, painted ladies:
extra blossoms adorning the buddleia.

Occasional refugees came for shelter,
like the overwintering tortoiseshell
clamped on top of the lavatory cistern
(I had to protect it from the plumber),

and another under the tread of a stair,
camouflaging its closed brown underwings
against the carpet, as if safe on bark.
Sometimes our house was just an extra tree.

The years deleted them. They've left only
one frayed wing in a bowl of foreign coins;
and the great dark moths have gone, that thudded
into the lamps in sulphurous heatwaves.

*

Instead I've been given this handsome corpse
from the butterfly house at Lancaster:
Papilio memnon agenor, male form –
the Great Mormon, with its five-inch wingspan,

black as a collage from a rook's feathers,
framed in a three-dimensional surround
from Paperchase, and sent to me by post.
I'd say it has a baleful look about it.

Bees' Nest

Bumble-, not honey-; and not a hive.
Ignore those trim little boxes, fitted
with a glass inner lid for viewing
and an entry tunnel of the right gauge,
in friends-of-the-planet catalogues.

Such things may do the trick for blue tits,
with their predictable minds. This bee
won't be invited into your parlour.
She'll build in your compost heap; she'll squat
in a disused mouse-hole; or she's

a cross noise buzzing inside the lawn
so that you desist from using clippers,
and an ever-larger moss-thatched skull
rises from the earth like the Green Man,
his head crowning, being slowly born.

With luck it will be in a summer
rich with visitors, so that a child
may find herself transfixed by a procession
of bees, all in the house uniform,
popping out of the grass, just like that,

to go browsing in the buddleia
or shove their snouts into yellow toadflax,
until they or their clone-kin zoom back
unerringly to the secret trapdoor
that gives access to their waxen dome.

But you worry that you haven't enough
flowers in your garden to feed them,
and that being more rare now they'll never
come back after this year's nest has sagged
into ruin. And they don't come back.

Dragonfly

In the next life I should like to be
for one perpetual day
a dragonfly: a series of blue-green
flashes over Lily Tarn,
a contraption of steel and cellophane
whose only verbs are dart, skim, hover.
One day is enough to remember.